The Making of a Champion

A World-Class Cricketer

Andrew Langley

www.heinemann.co.uk/library
Visit our website to find out more information about **Heinemann Library** books.

To order:
☎ Phone 44 (0) 1865 888066
▤ Send a fax to 44 (0) 1865 314091
▢ Visit the Heinemann Bookshop at www.heinemann.co.uk/library to browse our catalogue and order online.

First published in Great Britain by Heinemann Library, Halley Court, Jordan Hill, Oxford OX2 8EJ, part of Harcourt Education. Heinemann is a registered trademark of Harcourt Education Ltd.

Editorial: Geoff Barker, Rebecca Hunter and Dan Nunn
Design: Ian Winton
Illustrations: Peter Bull
Picture Research: Rachel Tisdale
Consultant: Jim Foulerton
Production: Duncan Gilbert

Originated by Ambassador Litho Ltd
Printed in China by WKT Company Limited

ISBN 0 431 18940 4
08 07 06 05 04
10 9 8 7 6 5 4 3 2 1

British Library Cataloguing in Publication Data
Langley, Andrew
 A world-class cricketer – (The making of a champion)
 1. Cricket – Juvenile literature
 2. Cricket – Training – Juvenile literature
 I. Title
 796.3'58
A full catalogue record for this book is available from the British Library.

Acknowledgements
The publishers would like to thank the following for permission to reproduce photographs:

Empics pp. **5 both**, 6, 7, 8, **11 bottom**, 14, 18, **19 both**, **21 both**, 22, 23, 26, **27 top**, 29, **30 both**, 32 (Chris Turvey), 35, 38, **39 top**, **41 top**, **43 top**, **43 bottom**; Getty Images pp. 4 (Hamish Blair), 9 (Michael Steele), 10 (Bryn Lennon), **13 top**, **15 top & 16** (Hamish Blair), 17 (Mike Hewitt), 24 (Hamish Blair), 25 (Darren England), **27 bottom** (Hamish Blair), 28 (Hamish Blair), 31 (Hamish Blair), 33, 34 (Touchline Photo), **36 top** (Tom Shaw), **36 bottom** (Hamish Blair), 37 (Ben Radford), **39 bottom** (Adrian Murrell), 40 (Laurence Griffiths), **41 bottom** (Jewel Samad), 42 (Adrian Murrell), **43 bottom** (Jewel Samad).

Cover photograph reproduced with permission of Hamish Blair/Getty Images.

Every effort has been made to contact copyright holders of any material reproduced in this book. Any omissions will be rectified in subsequent printings if notice is given to the publishers.

The paper used to print this book comes from sustainable resources.

Contents

Words printed in bold letters, **like these**, are explained in the Glossary.

Introducing cricket

The batsman takes a step down the wicket and whacks the ball high over the fielders for six. The fast bowler sends the stumps flying with a lightning fast yorker. The wicketkeeper leaps through the air to take a stunning one-handed catch. Cricket is full of explosive moments like these.

A world sport

Cricket is actually a very simple game. One player has a ball. Another has a bat to hit it. Out of this has grown one of the world's great sports, which is played in every continent (even Antarctica!). People play cricket in parks and streets, on village greens and beaches, as well as on famous Test grounds such as Lord's in London or Eden Gardens in Calcutta, India. Thousands go to see Test matches or one-day internationals, while millions more watch the games on television or listen to radio commentary.

Playing for the side

Unlike many other sports, cricket demands a wide range of skills. Batting and bowling are two entirely different crafts which need separate talents and training methods. Not many cricketers have been gifted enough to be brilliant at both! Then there is fielding, which can involve everything from throwing and catching to running, sliding and almost turning somersaults!

Above all, cricket is a team sport. Individual players are part of a team of eleven trying to win a match. When they field, all eleven are playing together to dismiss the opposition batters. When they bat, the batsman and his partner combine to score runs against eleven fielders. No one can win a match on their own. It takes a team effort, made up of bowling, batting and fielding.

Modern fielders have to be great athletes. Here, Brad Hogg of Australia dives to reach the ball.

Left-handed West Indian Brian Lara is one of the most brilliant and high-scoring batsmen in cricket history.

The demands of cricket

Some people think of cricket as being a slow game, which does not need much fitness or stamina. Try saying that to someone who has been batting for three hours, or to a fast bowler who has just completed twenty **overs**! A cricketer has to be very fit, and able to stay alert and energetic through a whole day on the field. Batters, bowlers and fielders have to concentrate on every ball bowled – because it might be coming their way. One moment (a catch, a **run out**, a perfect delivery) can change the course of a whole match.

Cricket can seem complicated. The rules (called 'laws') of the game have developed and changed over more than 100 years. Players are constantly working out new methods of getting the better of their opponents – new tactics, new types of delivery and even new bat strokes. All this means that there is a lot to learn. But it also adds to the special magic of cricket.

Even umpires get it wrong! Mark Ramprakash has got his bat in the crease as the ball thrown by the fielder hits the stumps – but he was still judged to be run out.

Village green to World Cup

Cricket is a very old game. One record shows that an English prince was playing something called 'creaget' over 700 years ago. Some people believe that the distance between **stumps** and the front **crease** (or **popping crease**) (now 1.22 metres) was originally measured out using an arrow. Cricket was certainly popular by the reign of Elizabeth I in the 1590s, and soon it was being played abroad.

Modern methods

The game of cricket as we now know it was born in Hambledon, a little village in Hampshire, in southern England. During the 1780s, the Hambledon team beat all comers – even county sides. Slowly, cricket became a national sport. The shape of the bat changed, three stumps were used instead of two and lawnmowers made better cricket pitches possible.

The greatest invention of all was roundarm bowling. Until the 1820s, the ball was bowled underarm. Then players found that they could bowl faster and better by swinging their arms round, and later, over the shoulder. (This method may have been invented by a woman, who was unable to bowl underarm because of her wide skirts.) Roundarm gave bowlers the chance to develop new weapons of swerve, bounce and spin.

William Gilbert Grace, known to the world as W. G. Grace, dominated English cricket during his long career between 1868 and 1904.

Sanath Jayasuriya

In 1996 Sri Lanka amazed and delighted cricket watchers by winning the World Cup. The main reason for their success was their rapid rate of scoring, which other teams could not match – and their fastest scorer was Sanath Jayasuriya. The short, left-handed batsman used his powerful forearms to hit the ball with enormous force, and played aggressively from the first ball. After this triumph, Jayasuriya established himself as one of the most destructive and feared batters in the world. His greatest **innings** of all was a massive 340 in his side's total of 952 against India in 1998.

Test cricket begins

Cricket grew up in Britain, but the game quickly took root in countries of the old British Empire such as Australia and India. In 1859 an English touring party boarded a ship for North America to play its first overseas match.

The first ever **Test match** was played on an England tour of Australia in 1877. So began a series of contests that have gone on ever since. By the 1950s, these original countries had been joined by South Africa, the West Indies, India, New Zealand and Pakistan. The first World Cup of **limited-overs** matches (currently 60 each side) took place in England in 1975. Since then several other countries from Africa and Asia have also gained Test match status.

Cricket timeline	
1859	First England cricket tour, to Canada and the USA
1865	W. G. Grace plays his debut first-class match
1877	First Test match: Australia v. England at Melbourne
1882	Australia beats England for the first time in England
1905	First Test match in South Africa
1909	ICC (Imperial Cricket Conference) is founded
1928	West Indies play their first Test match (in England)
1929	First Test match in New Zealand
1932	India play their first Test match (in England)
1935	First Women's Test match: New Zealand v. England
1952	Pakistan play their first Test match (in India)
1975	First One-Day World Cup (in England)
1982	First Test match in Sri Lanka
1989	ICC changes name to International Cricket Council
1996	First Test match in Zimbabwe
2000	First Test match in Bangladesh

Cricket around the world

Today, cricket is truly a world sport. The number of Test-playing nations continues to grow (with Bangladesh joining in 2000). Seven other teams were good enough to compete in the 2003 World Cup alongside the senior sides. The worldwide governing body, the ICC (International Cricket Council) set up a special Trophy competition in 1979 for non-Test countries.

Europe

England was the birthplace of cricket, and is still one of the major centres of the sport. Every cricketer dreams of appearing at Lord's, the most famous of all cricket grounds, and many overseas players come to Britain to play for the county sides or in the club leagues. Club cricket is also now played in many other European countries.

Asia

The Indian sub-continent is probably the most cricket-mad region in the world today. India's victory in the 1983 World Cup sparked a national mania for **limited-overs** cricket. Interest in Pakistan and Sri Lanka has also been boosted by World Cup wins. Bangladesh is the newest Test country, and several other Asian nations, including Malaysia and the United Arab Emirates, also play international cricket.

Women's cricket

Women have been playing cricket nearly as long as men. The first recorded match was in 1745 – and a woman is reputed to have invented roundarm bowling. The first women's cricket club, White Heather, was founded in 1887, and in 1935 an England team toured New Zealand. Since the 1970s, regular Test series have been played between England, Australia, India, the West Indies and other countries. Here, Auckland's wicketkeeper Katherine Round keeps a steady eye on the ball.

Africa

South Africa and Zimbabwe are the leading cricketing nations in Africa (though South Africa was barred from Tests between 1970 and 1994 because of its **apartheid** policy). Clubs in Namibia, Kenya and other East African countries are now developing quickly.

The Caribbean

The West Indies, with its flamboyant batters and express bowlers, was the world's most exciting team from the 1950s to the 1990s. Recent failures mean that cricket in the Caribbean is having to battle hard against the rival attraction of baseball.

Oceania

Australia has been at the top of the world rankings for several years, while the New Zealand side has had

A close fielder jumps out of the way as the ball whistles past during a game at the BKSP sports ground in Dhaka, Bangladesh, between Bangladesh A and the England touring team of 2003.

moments of dramatic success. Cricket is also making huge strides in the Pacific Islands, notably Fiji and Papua New Guinea.

North and South America

Canada won its first-ever World Cup finals game in 2003 when it defeated Bangladesh. The popularity of cricket has grown steadily, and there are now over 250 clubs in the country. Cricket has never really become popular in the USA, but in South America, there are long-established clubs in Chile, Brazil and Argentina.

Starting young

The earlier a cricketer begins to play the game, the better. Success in bowling, batting and fielding depends on technique almost as much as talent. If players learn the correct techniques right from the start, they can rely on them for the rest of their cricketing careers. Proper coaching will help technique enormously, too.

On the big stage: school cricketers take part in a Kwik Kricket game in the interval of a Test match at Trent Bridge, Nottingham.

Mini-cricket

The first lesson to learn is that cricket is fun. There are many simpler forms of the game specially aimed at showing young players just how enjoyable it can be. These have a less threatening soft ball in place of the hard leather one, and other easy-to-use equipment. These games are structured so that everyone gets a chance to bat and bowl (as well as field, of course).

One example is Kwik Kricket, pioneered in Britain. Players, from as young as five, use tennis balls and plastic bats and need no protective pads or gloves, while the **stumps** can be set up anywhere. Bowlers and batters are each given regular turns. Kanga is a game for slightly older children and is widely played in Australia. It uses wooden bats and special, semi-hard Kanga balls. All batters get two **overs** at the **crease**, no matter how often they are dismissed. There is also a marked zone behind the bowler's end where scores for hits are doubled.

Finding a team

If you live in a cricket-playing country, it should be easy to find a side to play for. Many schools have teams for pupils at all levels from seven or eight years old. Local clubs may have junior sides which are coached by senior players and compete in their own leagues. After school, keen cricketers can continue with the club into the senior teams. Colleges and employers may also organize teams – and provide practice facilities.

Cricket is a team game, and one of the most sociable of all sports. Team colleagues have to spend long hours together in the dressing room, on the **pavilion** balcony, on coaches to away matches, and of course on the field of play. So they must enjoy making friends and joining in. This will help build the team spirit which is a vital part of successful performances on the cricket field.

Youngsters in the Caribbean often start the game by playing beach cricket, using a soft ball and learning to deal with the waves!

Graham Gooch

As cricketers move into higher teams, they find themselves playing with better and more experienced players. They have to prove themselves each time they play. The

young Graham Gooch used to bat first for his local club, but when he was first picked for the Essex team he had to bat at number 9. By 1975 he had become a successful county cricketer and was selected to play for England. In his first Test match he batted at number 6 – and scored 0 and 0!

Equipment and clothing

Cricket needs more personal equipment than many other sports. Most of it is essential for all players and can be expensive, but it is important to buy good quality items which will not let you down.

Clothing and boots

The shirt and trousers should fit comfortably, without being too baggy. Long-sleeved shirts are recommended for colder climates such as England. Many players also wear a vest to soak up body sweat.

Professionals have more than one type of boot, which they will choose according to the weather and the condition of the surface. On a damp field, longer studs will help give a better grip. Fast- and medium-pace bowlers may wear tougher boots than fielders. These are fitted with shock-absorbing insoles, so that the boots can cope with the extra wear and tear caused by the stresses of the delivery strides.

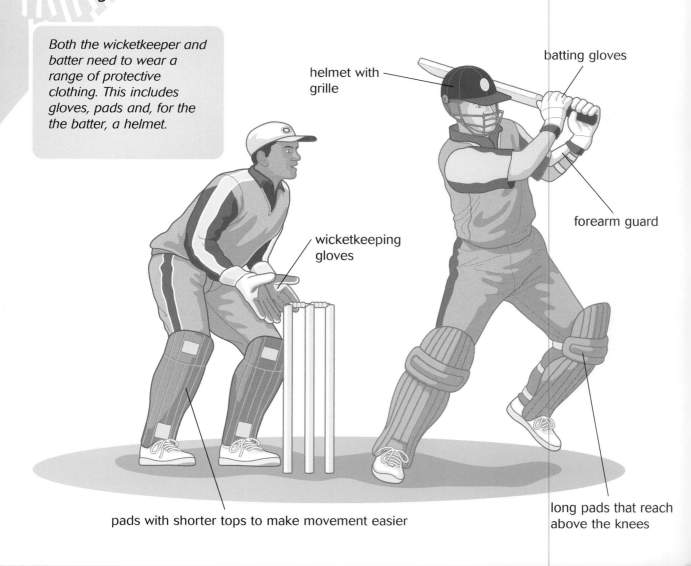

Both the wicketkeeper and batter need to wear a range of protective clothing. This includes gloves, pads and, for the the batter, a helmet.

helmet with grille

batting gloves

forearm guard

wicketkeeping gloves

pads with shorter tops to make movement easier

long pads that reach above the knees

Bats

The traditional bat is made of plain willow. A new bat must be prepared by treating it sparingly with linseed oil and then 'knocking it in' by gently tapping it with an old ball or a special mallet. This slowly toughens the surface. After use, the bat should be wiped off and any cracks gently sanded smooth. There is also a polyarmoured bat, which has a plastic coating over the wood. This type of bat needs no oiling or knocking in.

Nobody should use a bat that is too heavy for their size and strength, because this will reduce the flexibility and speed of their shot-taking. Modern Test batsmen tend to have heavier bats than those used in the 1950s and 1960s. They feel that this gives them greater power.

A bat maker at work in Nagpur, India. Note the different sizes of bat – from regular size to smaller ones for children.

Helmets *fact*

No one wore a batting helmet for the first 100 years of Test cricket. Occasionally, batsmen were hit by deliveries from quick bowlers. The most horrifying incident was when India's captain Nari Contractor suffered a fractured skull in Barbados in 1962. He was rushed to hospital and an emergency operation saved his life although his career was ended. Helmets were first worn in the late 1970s, partly in response to the ferocious pace of the West Indian attack at that time. Now most adult batters wear helmets when facing fast- or even medium-paced bowling.

Protecting yourself

Batting gloves should fit well but not tightly, and be easy to undo so that they can be slipped on and off quickly. Pads should cover the legs from the ankle to above the knee and be as light as possible, with straps tucked neatly out of the way. Male players must also wear a protective box for the groin area inside an athletic support.

Against quick bowling, batters wear pads on their front thigh and their chest. Some also put an arm guard on their leading forearm. Helmets are worn in club and first-class cricket, but are not really necessary for school or junior players.

Batting

Batting and bowling could be seen as the two sides of an argument. The bowler tries to get the batter out, and the batter tries to hit the ball away from the fielders and run between the **wickets** to score runs. Batting is a matter of reacting to deliveries and making decisions. A batter has to assess the speed, length and direction of the ball, select a shot to deal with it, and then execute the shot properly – all within about one second!

Batting basics

Some great batsmen are born with exceptional gifts. They have lightning-fast reflexes, superb co-ordination of hand and eye, and the natural ability to time a shot perfectly. Many others have less natural talent, but they can still improve their batting with regular practice and good coaching.

A batter must first learn to grip the cricket bat properly, with the hands close together near the top of the handle. The way the batter stands at the **crease** should be well balanced, with the front shoulder pointing at the bowler, and the eyes level.

Selecting a shot

As the ball is bowled, the batter first decides whether to play back or forward. This depends on the length of the delivery. Generally, if the ball is bowled to bounce well short of the batter, the batter moves back to play the shot, and if it is pitched well up, the batter moves forward.

Next, the batter must choose the correct shot, either to defend the wicket or to score runs. There is a wide range of strokes to play, from the defensive 'block' to the attacking **drive** (hitting with a vertical swing of the bat), or pull (hitting to the **leg side** with a horizontal bat).

Indian batsman Rahul Dravid has a perfect stance as he waits for the ball to be delivered. He is balanced and relaxed, with his head held straight and steady.

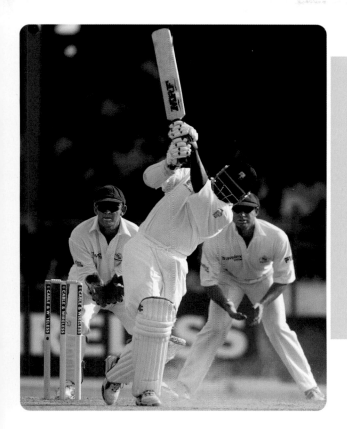

Brian Lara

West Indian Brian Lara is one of the greatest modern batsmen, and holds the record for the highest first-class score (501). As a small boy, he practised his shots for hours on the front porch of his home, using a broom handle as a bat and a marble as a ball. He arranged the flower pots to represent fielders and tried to hit the marble through the gaps between them.

Each stroke has its own technique, and needs extensive practice. Once the basics are learned, this can be done in front of a mirror, where the batter can check that the details are correct. Top players such as England's Michael Vaughan and India's Sachin Tendulkar are especially good at their shot selection.

Building an innings

A successful **innings** will probably last at least an hour. The batter has time to play himself in and get used to the light, the atmosphere and the pace of the wicket. The key to a long innings is the ability to concentrate completely on each ball as it is bowled. Many great players are able to 'switch off' between deliveries, and then switch on again as the bowler runs in.

The batter prepares to receive a ball from the bowler. He must judge the line and length, and choose a suitable stroke to play – all in a split second.

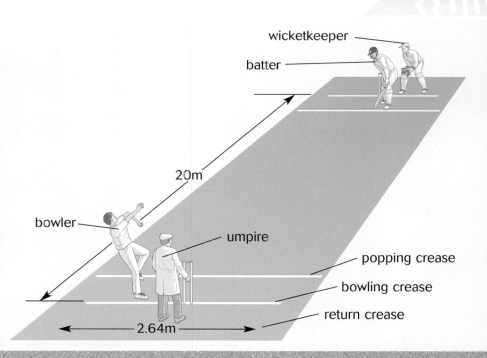

wicketkeeper

batter

20m

bowler

umpire

popping crease

bowling crease

return crease

2.64m

Fast bowling

Bowlers win matches. Batters try to score as many runs as they can, but a side only wins when it gets the opposition out – and that's the job of the bowlers. The fast bowlers are the shock troops of the side, who aim to dismiss opponents through speed and bounce. But pace bowling is very hard work, needing fitness and stamina. A bowler who has bowled 20 **overs** will have sprinted well over a mile simply by running up to the **crease**!

Bowling basics

Most great fast bowlers are athletic as well as strong, and have a balanced, rhythmical action. This rhythm begins with the run-up, which should not be too long. It builds up at the crease, with the delivery stride and the action of releasing the ball. And it finishes with the follow-through (the continuation of the action after the ball is bowled), which helps maintain momentum and absorbs some of the impact of the action.

Quick bowlers come in all sizes. Recent English players illustrate this.

Some are short, like Darren Gough, and can 'skid' the ball through. Very tall bowlers (like Steve Harmison) use their extra height to get greater bounce. Sometimes a bowler depends on very strong arms and shoulders for extreme pace (like, for example, Andrew Flintoff).

All eleven members of the fielding Australian Test side can be seen here. Seven stand in a line to the right of the wicketkeeper hoping for the batter to give away a catch off a fast delivery from the bowler, Brett Lee.

Fastest of the fast

Who was the quickest bowler of all time? Over the years, men like Wes Hall and Frank 'Typhoon' Tyson were given this title. But before the days of devices that can measure the speed of the ball, called speed guns, it was impossible to measure exactly how fast a delivery was. Recently Pakistan's Waqar Younis and Australia's Brett Lee have bowled at over 153 kph (94 mph). But only one bowler has bowled a delivery to crack the magic 160 kph (100 mph) mark – Shoaib Akhtar of Pakistan (right).

Fast bowler's armoury

Speed is a powerful weapon, but very few bowlers are naturally quick enough to use it consistently. Much more important is control of line and length. A good length ball should make it hard for the batter to decide whether to play back or forward. A good line is usually on or just outside the **off stump**. South Africa's Shaun Pollock is not as fast as many bowlers, but he bowls a very good line and length that means batters have to take more risks to score runs off him.

Swing fact

Why does a cricket ball swing in the air? Nobody knows for certain, but most people believe it is governed by the shiny nature of the ball. Swing bowlers try to keep one side of the ball shiny, by rubbing it on this side, and let the other side go dull. They then deliver the ball so that the seam is upright. The theory is that the shiny side will travel quicker than the dull side, causing the ball to curve as it flies.

The next step is to make the ball change direction after it has left the bowler's hand. This can be done by making use of the ball's 'seam', the stitching which makes a narrow ridge round its middle. By pitching it on the seam, a bowler can cause it to move off line. Bowlers can also make the ball 'swing' in the air, either away from the batter or (more difficult) into the batter (see Swing fact).

Like any other cricketer, a fast bowler needs to bowl a variety of deliveries. A fast **bouncer**, pitched half-way down the **wicket**, can unsettle a batter by jumping head-high. A **yorker**, pitched in line with the batter's feet, can get under the bat. And a slower ball can ruin the batter's timing.

Spin bowling

A slow spin bowler can be just as dangerous as a fast bowler. Instead of speed and swing, slow bowlers use cunning and deceit to defeat the batter. They need the same basic techniques of a balanced run-up and delivery stride and a proper follow-through, and must maintain good line and length. But they also have an extra weapon – flight. By tossing the ball higher so that it stays longer in the air, they are also giving it more chance to spin.

Off-break

An off-break is a delivery that spins from the **off side** to the **leg side**. The bowler holds the ball across the seam, and cocks the wrist when going into the delivery stride. As the ball is released, the wrist flicks forward and the first and second fingers are dragged down the right-hand side. This sets the ball spinning, so that it will turn in towards the batter when it bounces.

This is the standard delivery of the off-spinner. There are many ways of adding variety to the bowler's attack. He or she can deceive the batter with

a ball that does not spin at all. Or the length, height and speed of the delivery can be altered to unsettle the opponent. For example, India's Harbhajan Singh is renowned for his ability to vary the pace and length of his bowling.

The magic of Muralitharan

Sri Lanka's Muttiah Muralitharan is one of the greatest spin bowlers in cricket history. His off-breaks have brought him over 500 victims in around 90 **Test matches**. He is able to give the ball an amazingly ferocious twist thanks to his extraordinary right arm. 'Murali' was born with a permanently bent elbow and a double-jointed wrist. This allows him to make the ball spin and bounce more than any other bowler currently playing Test cricket.

Leg break

A leg break spins from the leg side to the off side. This is a much more difficult type of delivery to bowl than an off-break, because the wrist and fingers have to move to the left rather than the right of the ball. This is a less natural motion, and means that the bowler will have his body in a more 'square-on' position with his chest facing down the **wicket**, when the ball is released. For this reason, the leg break is harder to control.

However, batters also find leg-spin more difficult because the ball is spinning across them rather than into them. Clever leg-spinners can make use of their more strained action by mixing in special trick balls. The most famous of these is the 'googly'. This appears to be delivered just like a leg break, but spins the other way. Then there is the 'flipper', which spins directly forwards, not turning at all but gathering pace after it bounces. Australia's Shane Warne is a master of all these variations.

This picture of Indian leg break bowler Anil Kumble shows how much effort goes into the body action during a delivery.

Australian spinner Shane Warne (without cap) celebrates with his teammates after taking a wicket with an amazing delivery.

Fielding and keeping wicket

During a match, cricketers spend most of their time fielding. Not everyone bowls and sometimes not everyone bats – but everyone has to field. It is the most basic of cricketing skills and something every player should spend a lot of time practising. Good aggressive and alert fielding encourages bowlers and puts pressure on batters.

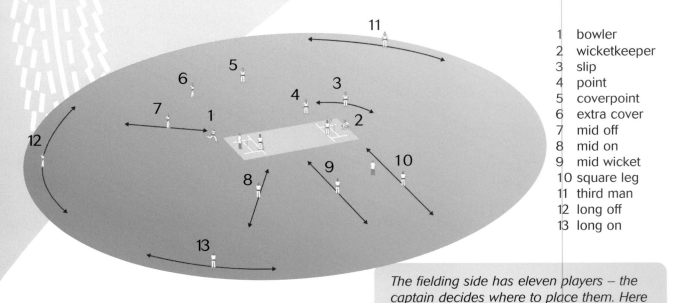

1	bowler
2	wicketkeeper
3	slip
4	point
5	coverpoint
6	extra cover
7	mid off
8	mid on
9	mid wicket
10	square leg
11	third man
12	long off
13	long on

The fielding side has eleven players – the captain decides where to place them. Here thirteen typical fielding positions are shown.

Fielding basics

To stop a hard-hit shot, the fielder should always try to get his or her body behind the ball. They will put one knee on the ground across the path of the shot and the other foot next to it, and hold the palms of the hands open ready to receive the ball. When chasing a ball, the right-handed fielder should pick it up with the outside of the right foot next to it.

Fielders close to the **wicket** should always be alert to running the batters out by hitting the **stumps** with the ball when one of them is out of the **crease**. Picking up and throwing quickly are essential parts of attacking fielding. Fielders should perform the pickup so that the body is in the correct position for an immediate throw. The thrower should aim for the top of the stumps.

'Catches win matches' is an old saying, but true. Again, practice will improve technique, reflexes and the co-ordination of hand and eye. As with other cricket skills, the first rule for a player is to keep his head still and watch the ball. Fielders, whether near the bat or near the boundary, must learn to cope with both high and low catches, and those that drop behind them or far in front.

Jonty Rhodes

Jonty Rhodes was simply the most spectacular fielder in modern cricket – possibly ever. He was able to stop, catch and throw the ball in ways that seemed impossible. Rhodes first hit the headlines in the 1992 World Cup, when he dived straight into the stumps, ball in hand, to run out Inzamam-ul-Haq of Pakistan. Since then he dismissed many batters and saved his side hundreds of runs (some watchers calculate that he saved South Africa at least 40 runs in every **innings**). This is not just the result of talent. Rhodes was renowned for the hours of hard work he put into his fielding practice.

Behind the stumps

The wicketkeeper is in the thick of the action, taking balls that pass the bat, and collecting throws from fielders. He or she has more chances of taking wickets too, from catches, stumpings or run outs. A lively and efficient keeper such as England's Jack Russell can inspire a fielding side. The way a keeper stands is vital.

Most keepers squat down and rise as the ball is played. To take fast bowling, they stand some distance behind the stumps, but for slow bowlers they stand very close. Watching the ball is especially important for a keeper – but much more difficult, because the delivery is often masked by the movements of the batsman.

A throw from a fielder hits the stumps and Pakistan's Saeed Anwar is run out during a World Cup game in 2003.

Coaching

Cricketers cannot learn on their own. They need someone else outside the team who will analyse their performance, plan schedules and give advice and encouragement. This person is the coach. He or she may be a retired cricketer, although the best players do not necessarily make the best coaches. A good coach needs to understand all aspects of the game, to be able to communicate well with the players, and to have clear and positive goals.

Coaching skills

Major sides usually have a large coaching staff, under the control of the senior coach. There should be a specialist coach for each area of skill – batting, the different styles of bowling, wicketkeeping and fielding – as well as fitness. They will all work out their own drills for practising, improving technique and solving practical problems.

Of course, not every player needs intensive coaching. Some have their own natural style which works effectively – even sensationally! For example, the West Indian all-rounder Gary Sobers never had any coaching at all. Yet he became one of the greatest batsmen in Test history, setting many records (including highest Test score, most runs and the

Duncan Fletcher

England coach Duncan Fletcher (left) was never a star player. He was born in Zimbabwe and had his cricket career before his country joined the Test-playing nations. Yet after retiring he showed that he was an exceptional coach, first with his old side Western Province, and then Glamorgan, in Wales. In 1999 he became the first ever overseas coach of the England team. Within a few years he had transformed its fortunes, taking it from the bottom of the table to third in the world rankings. Quiet and reserved, Fletcher emphasized the importance of teamwork and putting constant pressure on the opposing players. He gave personal attention to individual team members, and pushed for the selection of fresh and unusual players such as Marcus Trescothick.

Children learn the techniques of catching from a coach at Surrey County Cricket Club's indoor school.

first batter to hit 6 'sixes' in an over) and ending with an average batting score of nearly 58. In cases like this, the wise coach does not try to change the player's basic technique.

Coaching attitude

A coach is not there simply to sharpen up cricketing skills. His or her job includes sharpening the players' attitude and discipline on the field. Each member of the side should be given goals to achieve during a season, both in performance and development. These help to motivate the players and also offer them something solid to aim for.

The team's performance as a unit is just as important. The chief coach will be involved in everything from selecting the eleven and deciding on tactics, to mental preparation before walking on to the field. It is vital to create an atmosphere in which players will encourage and support each other.

The Australian Cricket Academy

The Australian Cricket Academy (ACA) was set up in 1987 as a school for preparing the country's best young players for the tough realities of life in first-class cricket. Based in Adelaide, the academy gives students two six-week blocks of intensive training. The courses cover not only skills and fitness, but are also about personal development and building a life outside cricket. They also include scientific subjects such as biomechanics and physiology. Over 30 ex-ACA members have played for Australia, notably Glenn McGrath, Jason Gillespie, Ricky Ponting and Brett Lee.

Fielding practice

Fielding practice often gets neglected by cricketers. Yet it is just as important as batting or bowling, and cricketers should spend just as much time doing it. There are now many different routines for developing fielding skills which involve large groups of players. These give scope for a huge variety of running, stopping and throwing actions and get the players used to communicating with each other on the field.

Stopping and throwing

The usual drill for outfielding is for someone to hit the ball in turn round a ring of fielders, who pick it up and throw it back. For close fielding, it may be more fun to play a game rather like football or hockey, called 'field ball'. Each team has a narrow goal (guarded by a goalkeeper) and a penalty area. Players score by rolling a ball past the keeper into the goal from outside the area, using only their weaker arms. They can pass, but not run with, the ball.

Fielders should practise overarm and underarm throwing. One of the secrets of good throwing is a strong and flexible wrist movement. This can be improved by players sitting in pairs and flicking the ball to each other, using only wrist and finger power. To stop their forearms moving, the players grip their wrist with their free hand. This exercise can be altered slightly to include the whole forearm, by gripping the upper arm.

Australian coach John Buchanan (left) runs a special drill for fielding practice with two players.

A New Zealand fielder dives in vain to stop a ball from crossing the boundary rope at the edge of the playing area.

Catching

All players practise catching in the deep (far away from the **wicket**). This is most easily done by hitting or throwing catches to each other, making sure that the speed and angle of the ball is varied each time. Top players concentrate on the basic catching skills – getting into line with the ball, watching it all the way, and cushioning the impact with elbows and shoulders.

Close catchers (those who stand close to the batsman) must get used to jumping and diving safely. Fielders can practise this in pairs, standing opposite each other with mats on either side.

They throw catches to each other over the mats, gradually making the catcher dive further and further. South Africa's Paul Adams and New Zealand's Stephen Fleming are both outstandingly athletic close catchers.

Wicketkeeping

Keepers have different skills to practise than other members of the side. These include taking the ball behind the wicket, catching **edged balls** and making stumpings. Rhythm, concentration and neat footwork are the keys to these skills, and can be improved by simple exercises. A bat is laid down on the spot where a good length delivery should pitch, and a player throws balls to bounce near it. The keeper has to catch the ball, and the bat helps him get used to the idea of a batter getting in his line of sight.

In the nets

Net practice is a crucial part of a cricketer's training. The nets are not the place to have a light-hearted slog. For a start, they can be dangerous, because people easily forget to concentrate on the balls flying about. Sloppy net routines can also get a player into bad and lazy habits, so batting and bowling there should be taken as seriously as in a proper match.

Batters

Nets are the ideal place for a coach to inspect a player's technique from close range. He or she will be able to spot weaknesses in technique and therefore get the batter to repeat the shot over and over until it is correct. This process can be helped greatly by having to bowl a specific kind of delivery, or by having a bowling machine which can be pre-set.

To make this simpler, only half the net length need be used. The bowler stands 5 to 10 metres from the batting **crease** and throws balls to the batter, either underarm or overarm. This exercise can be adapted to improve the batter's head and body position.

Botham in the nets

Ian Botham, probably the finest of England's all-rounders (a player who is good at both batting and bowling), often treated net practice as an opportunity to lose as many balls as possible by whacking them into the far distance. But as a youngster he had been rigorously taught the correct techniques of batting and bowling – something that made a huge difference to his career. In the school nets, his teacher would put a pile of coins on a good length, and the first bowler to hit them could have them. Botham got plenty of pocket money this way!

Australian coach John Buchanan uses a bowling machine to send a practice delivery at a batter during training in South Africa in February, 2003.

Batters in the nets can also use drills to improve their concentration and ball-watching skills. Australian coaches encourage the 'now' technique: when the bowler is about to deliver the ball, the batter says 'Now!' to himself, and this makes him concentrate. Ball-watching involves studying the angle and spin direction of the seam as the ball approaches. This helps to identify which way it might swing or turn.

Bowlers

Bowlers should use the nets to iron out any problems with their actions. First there is the run-up. Bowlers who persistently bowl no-balls by landing their feet in the wrong place, or who are unbalanced at the **wicket**, can make adjustments to their run-up length. Then there is the delivery action to be examined, especially the closeness to the **stumps**, the angle of the arm and the position at follow-through.

Line and length – the two key elements of good bowling – can also be practised in a fresh way. The narrow shape of a net tends to make it easier for bowlers to be accurate. But they should also focus on a good length, perhaps by laying down a marker (even a stump) at the ideal spot, and trying to hit it.

England batsmen train in the nets at Lord's Cricket Ground in London.

Fitness

Test cricketers today are much fitter than they have ever been. This improvement can be seen most clearly in the field, where speed, reaction times, athleticism and sheer physical commitment have changed hugely since the 1980s.

Brian Lara (centre) and the rest of the West Indian team warm up during training before a Test match in 2000.

On the road and in the gym

The benefits of fitness are obvious, and make it possible for players to perform at their best for longer periods. Fitness training is aimed at increasing a person's stamina, flexibility, speed and strength, and programmes will contain a combination of drills to develop all of these areas. These include total body exercises such as swimming and road running, repeat routines such as pull-ups and press-ups, sprinting sessions and training with weights.

Warming up and down

Cricketers should never start a match (or even a net practice) from cold. They should spend at least 20 minutes warming up before exercise to improve flexibility and prepare the joints, heart and muscles for action. This involves stretching the various sets of muscles in turn, and gently bending key areas such as the backbone and the hamstrings (the tendons at the back of the knees). After the game, at least 10 minutes should be spent in a cooling down routine to help the recovery of the blood system and muscles.

Nutrition

In a world of fat- and sugar-soaked fast food, young players must learn the importance of healthy eating. Types of food should be carefully chosen for their nutritional value, with special emphasis given to fresh, high-quality meat, fish and vegetables. Other 'good' foods, such as nuts, dried fruit and oat bars, will provide extra energy throughout a long day's play. Some coaches will even map out controlled diets for their players.

Cricket is usually played for long periods in very warm conditions. Players must take care to keep their fluid levels topped up, or they will suffer from cramps and tiredness. This does not simply mean drinking when they are very thirsty. It is best to drink regularly through the day. Water remains the best thirst-quencher of all, though fruit juice or high-energy sports drinks are also acceptable. The recommended intake is about 2.5 litres of water a day.

Alec Stewart

Former England cricketer Alec Stewart (centre) was one of the oldest of modern international players. He played his first Test in 1990 at the relatively late age of 26. Since then he appeared in over 120 more, often taking on the taxing double role of wicketkeeper and opening batsman (as well as captain in fifteen of them). He was still England's first choice keeper until his retirement from international cricket in 2003 at the age of 40. The major reason for his amazingly long career was his complete dedication to fitness and an ultra-healthy lifestyle.

Injuries

Every sportsperson will suffer some sort of injury during their career. Some injuries can be avoided – but others cannot. Cricket may not be a physical contact sport, but it still contains plenty of dangerous elements, notably a hard leather ball travelling at speeds of up to 160 kph (100 mph)! This has broken countless bones and even caused the death of several cricketers, though never yet in a **Test match**.

A fast low delivery strikes the sidepiece and grille of a batter's helmet.

Impact injuries

The cricket ball can cause a range of injuries, from bruising to fractures. For this reason, it is vital for batters, wicketkeepers and some close fielders to wear the correct protective clothing. Fielders can also injure themselves badly by falling awkwardly or running into each other. One Test player even managed to dislocate a shoulder by running into an advertising hoarding on the boundary. There are many treatments to speed up recovery from bruises, but fractured bones must be strapped or splinted in the normal way and given sufficient time to knit together properly.

Here, the England physiotherapist has rushed on to the field to look after batter Graham Thorpe, who has collapsed with a twisted back.

Strains and other dangers

Modern players are very fit, with bodies tuned to a high standard. However, this can make them more prone to injury, because they are frequently pushing themselves to the limit. Fast bowlers are especially at risk, because they repeat the same strenuous movement time after time, putting great pressure on their legs and feet. Ice packs and anti-inflammatory medicines are among the most frequent treatments for swellings, while ultrasound is used to heal strains and sprains.

Preventing injuries

A professional cricket team will have a fully qualified physiotherapist who will treat injuries and strains. But the coach and players themselves should make every effort to stop these occurring in the first place. On top of the usual fitness training, a sensible programme of 'conditioning' drills (including running, throwing and bowling) keeps the body match-fit. A good coach keeps a record of the injuries and other physical problems of his or her players.

Injuries facts

- Dennis Lillee, the top Australian pace bowler of the 1970s, wore a metal brace to help mend stress fractures of his lower spine, and returned to claim 300 more Test wickets.

- Michael Atherton, former England batsman and captain, had bone grafts to overcome spinal stress fractures, but played in pain for many of his 115 Test matches.

- The Australian spin bowler Shane Warne's chest-on, open leg-spinner's action caused him severe shoulder strain which required lengthy surgery. He came back in 1998 to reclaim his place as the world's best slow bowler.

- Simon Jones, English pace bowler, snapped knee ligaments in 2003 while sliding to field a ball in a Test match. He managed to overcome this career-threatening injury to be ready for Test selection a year later.

Being outside under the hot sun all day can be dangerous to health. Players should wear sunblock cream and a wide-brimmed hat to keep out the direct rays. Two hats, like Australian Martin Love is wearing, are even better!

Compete!

Matches in any sport can be won by mind as well as body. The greatest cricketers are not just the most talented, but those who most want to win. They will never give up a game until the final ball, and will always support their teammates. Some players can dominate their opponents through sheer confidence and strength of personality. This level of motivation should be encouraged from an early age, and built up as part of regular training.

Know your enemy

Careful study of the opposition is almost as important in cricket as determination. A good cricketer must have a sharp eye and a quick brain to find weaknesses in the other team. This is a vital skill for bowlers, who should be able to spot the areas where a batter is uncomfortable. Some dislike short-pitched deliveries, while others do not like playing balls outside the **off stump**. Many hitters get impatient if they are prevented from scoring.

Modern coaches use video recordings and computer analysis to pinpoint these faults. A player's actions can be watched many times, and special tactics worked out to exploit any weak points. This technology is also used to examine problem areas in their own side's batters and bowlers.

Even the best players can get better. Former England captain Michael Atherton studies a video of his practice session in the nets to look for faults.

Discipline

One Australian coaching maxim is: 'win with class and lose with grace'. Bad losers will find that their own performances suffer, and players who lose their temper will also lose concentration and focus. Dropped catches, umpiring mistakes and plain bad luck should be accepted and then put aside. It may be harder to ignore 'sledging' – degrading

remarks by opposition fielders, but this is a sad reality of today's cricket (especially at first-class level).

The umpire

The **umpire** has a very hard job. Many decisions, such as being called out for leg before wicket – when the ball strikes the batter on the pad in front of the **stumps** – depend on a variation of a few millimetres. It is not surprising that mistakes are made, although a good umpire will be respected even if he or she makes the occasional incorrect decision.

Leading a team

The captain of a cricket side has a huge influence on how a match is played (unlike a football captain, for instance). A powerful personality able to make positive decisions can change the course of a game. Managing people is the other key ingredient. Players should be given encouragement and only criticized in a positive way, so as to bring out the best in them.

Off the field

The captain's first task is to help in selecting the team. Captains are in the best position to judge a player's form and skill, and will choose team members who fit in with their own strategy. The batting order also needs careful thought, and can be altered to suit the immediate needs of the game.

The team spends a lot of time in the dressing room. For Test stars, this is often the only place where they can

Although he was one of the youngest players in the team, Graeme Smith (right) was appointed captain of South Africa in 2003. Here he leads his team off the field after a crushing victory over Bangladesh.

have complete privacy and freedom, away from the public and media. All players should be able to relax and give honest opinions here. The captain should keep an eye on the atmosphere in the dressing room and move quickly to stop problems.

On the field

It takes luck to win the toss at the start of a match, but intelligence and experience to decide whether to take first **innings**. Most captains will bat first as this means the opposition will have to bat later when the pitch is likely to be worn and rough. However, if the pitch is damp and weather conditions suit the swing bowlers, some captains choose to field first.

The placing of the fielders is a crucial skill. Make the field too attacking, and a captain may give away cheap runs. Make it too defensive, and the captain may miss the chance of taking **wickets**. The captain should always be prepared to alter his fielders' positions – if only to keep them alert. India's Sourav Ganguly is a shrewd judge of when to move fielders close to the batsman to increase the pressure on him and encourage him to make mistakes.

Imaginative bowling changes also make a big difference to the state of a game. Variety in the speed and style of the bowling can unsettle a batter. Fast bowlers should be used in short bursts, and even slow bowlers need a rest. The captain must make sure that his bowlers know his plans, and what line he wants them to bowl.

Inspiring captain

Mike Brearley (right) was an average batsman but an exceptional captain, who led England for a second spell in the Test series against the Australians in 1981. His side was already 0–1 down, and his leading player, Ian Botham, was in bad form and low spirits. Brearley knew exactly how to get Botham fired up again: he asked him if he wanted to be dropped from the team! Stung by this, Botham played one of the great Test innings (149 not out) in the next match at Headingley, enabling England to grab an astonishing victory. In the next Test, Brearley made fun of Botham's new bowling style. Botham went back to his old technique and won the match with a spell of 5 wickets for 1 run.

Regional cricket

So how does a young cricketer move on to become a top player? The next step after schools or local cricket is into a district team. This may be a county (in England), an island (in the West Indies) or a state (in South Africa). It is also the big step into the first-class game, where the best cricketers in the world make their living. This is often a difficult time for young players, who have become used to being the top performers at a lower level, and now find themselves at the bottom again.

Playing full time

Once they have been taken on by a regional side, promising young cricketers usually work their way up by playing for under-19 teams and second teams. Those with special talents may be selected to attend

Stars of the future? England's Nasser Hussain coaches budding cricketers at Port Elizabeth, South Africa.

cricket training establishments, such as the various sports academies in different countries.

In most countries, the first-class players are professionals – they are paid, and cricket is their full-time job. This means that they must be committed to the game as their career, and prepared to put aside other plans. Sport is not a very secure kind of employment, so anyone who becomes professional has to have courage and self-belief.

The Queen's Park Stadium in Grenada, West Indies has a lush and relaxed setting.

However, there are plenty of advantages. Most modern full-time cricketers are well paid, and there are opportunities for 'perks' such as sponsored cars, clothing and equipment. They also have much more opportunity for skills and fitness training, with the best of coaching and facilities.

Four-day to one-day

First-class players have to get used to much longer matches than they will have experienced before, played over three or four days. Club matches usually last only one day, with each side having one **innings**. In four-day matches each side has two. Players will need to develop greater stamina and new tactics to last the pace, either in building a long innings or in bowling long spells on consecutive days.

Regional cricket now features a huge variety of competitions. Besides the four-day league games, there are several kinds of **limited-overs** matches. English county cricketers, for example, play in four different one-day cup contests. Two of these

are 50 **overs** per side and one is 40 overs per side. The latest is 20/20, which was introduced in 2003 and allows each side only 20 overs each.

Domestic contests fact

Each major cricketing country has its own regional competitions. Some are one-day contests with each side having a limited number of overs. Others (shown below) include full-length matches over three or four days. The teams play in leagues.

Country	Competition
Australia	Sheffield Shield (6 states)
Bangladesh	National Cricket League (6 regional sides)
England	County Championship (18 counties, divided into 2 divisions)
India	Ranji Trophy (28 regional sides)
New Zealand	Shell Trophy (6 districts)
Pakistan	Qaid-e-Azam Trophy (8 districts)
South Africa	Currie Cup (6 states)
Sri Lanka	Premier League (16 regional sides)
West Indies	Red Stripe Cup (6 districts or islands)
Zimbabwe	Logan Cup (4 regional sides)

World Cup

The finals of the World Cup are the biggest event in the cricketing calendar, and playing there is one of the dreams of every ambitious cricketer. It takes place every four years, and is hosted by different countries or regions in turn. The ten Test-playing nations take part automatically, and four other teams reach the finals by coming through a series of qualifying rounds. The 2003 finals lasted for seven weeks and included 54 matches.

A different game

Of course, the World Cup is not about five-day Test matches, but one-day cricket (of 50 **overs** per side). Specialist tactics and skills are needed to excel in this form of the game – batters who can invent shots, bowlers who prevent run-scoring and brilliant ground fielders. Most countries select some players for their World Cup squads who may not even be regulars in Tests. Australia's Michael Bevan is an outstanding example of a superb **limited-overs** cricketer who rarely plays in **Test matches**.

Michael Bevan

Australian Michael Bevan is not an outstanding Test batsman. His average is about 30 runs per innings – much too low to gain him a regular place in the Australian Test side. However, he is the star of the national team in limited-overs cricket, and has been rated as the world's best one-day batsman. In over 200 games, he scored over 6000 runs at an average of more than 54 (the highest in his team).

His calmness in a crisis and his ability to score steadily have taken Australia to many important victories when all seemed lost. Among these was the World Cup semi-final against South Africa in 1999, when Australia were in trouble at 68 for 4 **wickets**. Bevan did not panic but scored a precious 65, and his team went on to win.

Cup history

The very first Cricket World Cup, staged in England in 1973, was for women's teams. The World Cup for men did not get going until 1975, also in England. Several non-Test teams took part, including one representing East Africa. Here the West Indies, with their thrilling batting and fielding and superb fast bowling, won easily. Much the same happened in 1979, which marked Canada's first appearance.

The third competition, in 1983, included Zimbabwe for the first time. It also produced a huge surprise when India won an amazing victory over the West Indies in the final. This caused an explosion of interest in one-day cricket in the sub-continent. The 1987 World Cup, won by Australia, was held in India.

The Australians hosted the 1991 finals which produced another first-time winner – Pakistan. Sri Lanka took the cup in 1995 in Lahore.

Catches win matches: Sachin Tendulkar (left) and Yuvraj Singh celebrate a wicket for India during the 2003 World Cup.

The Indian team astonished everyone by winning the 1983 World Cup final at Lord's in London.

Since then Australia has been in charge, with easy victories in England (1999) and South Africa (2003). The competition has now expanded to include 14 teams, among them non-Test nations, who have included Holland, the United Arab Emirates, Namibia and Kenya.

Test cricket

A **Test match** is the peak of cricket, both for watchers and for players. At its best, it is an exciting drama that can last for five days, with first one side in control, then the other. Over such a long period, strategy and stamina can play an enormous part.

Coping with the pressure

Test matches demand a lot more of players than even first-class cricket. For a start, there is the emotional pressure. The Test squad usually meets three days before the game to sharpen their skills in the nets, discuss tactics and bond together as a team. This can be a difficult time for new players, as they will be mixing with cricketers who already have big reputations and a lot of experience. Tension is built up further by media coverage in the press, TV and radio.

Playing in front of a huge, noisy crowd, such as the one here in Mohali, India, requires strong nerves and great concentration.

Then there is the size of the crowd. Big arenas such as the Melbourne Cricket Ground in Australia can hold up to 100,000 people. Lahore in Pakistan and Ahmedabad in India are almost as large, and the spectators make even more noise. Making a debut in front of so many people can be a terrifying experience.

Mental and physical toughness

Five days of cricket can put an immense strain on the body as well as the mind. A batter's two **innings** might last for eight or ten hours, and a bowler might send down 70 or more **overs**. Players cannot be replaced (except for fielding), and so injuries have to be ignored if possible. West Indian fast bowler Malcolm Marshall once played on with a broken arm in plaster and took seven **wickets**!

Much of a Test cricketer's time is spent away from home. He may play in six or more internationals in a home season (not to mention one-day matches). Players picked for an

England cricketers pose in front of the famous Taj Mahal in Agra during a tour of India in 1993.

overseas tour will then spend another three months or even longer travelling to distant countries. Ambitious cricketers have to be prepared for such long absences from home.

Saqlain Mushtaq

Slow bowler Saqlain Mushtaq made his debut for Pakistan at the age of 19, and took a wicket with his seventh ball in international cricket. Up to 2003 he took over 200 wickets in 47 Test matches, and is regarded as the best off-spin bowler in the world. He is very difficult to hit away for runs, and his 'mystery' ball can baffle even the best batters. This is a delivery which he causes to drift or float away in the air from a right-handed batsman. Saqlain has also taken nearly 300 wickets in **limited-overs** internationals.

Being a champion

The world's leading cricketers are celebrities. They are recognized in the street, interviewed widely and offered big sponsorship deals. They may appear on television shows and write newspaper columns. In cricket-mad countries like India or Sri Lanka they may even have their own fan clubs. All this fame helps to build up the pressure on players to go on performing to very high standards.

Staying at the top

An international player's career may last for ten years, and stretch over more than 100 games. Gary Sobers, the great West Indian all-rounder, played from 1954 to 1974, but at that time there were many fewer matches in a year. Only a very good cricketer can last that long.

The main challenge is to maintain fitness and form. Constant wear and tear on hard pitches may cause lasting damage to bowlers' knee and hip joints, and wicket keepers can suffer from battered fingers and hands. It takes enormous dedication to keep on with punishing fitness programmes year after year.

Tendulkar's amazing achievements

Even when he was a boy, it was obvious that India's Sachin Tendulkar was going to be a batting genius. At school his average number of runs per **innings** was 1034! He was invited to attend nets with the Indian Test team at the age of 14. He scored centuries in his first innings in each of the three major competitions in India, and made his first Test hundred in 1990 when he was only 16. In 1992 he became the youngest player to reach 1000 Test runs. By 2003, he had taken his total to nearly 9000 in just over 100 matches, with 31 centuries, and will probably go on to become the top run-scorer in Test history. Sachin Tendulkar is a major celebrity in his homeland, and everyone expects him to perform miracles every time he walks to the wicket.

Former international hero Ian Botham (right) gives expert comments during coverage of a Test match.

End of a career

Very few Test cricketers play internationals after the age of 40, and many retire from first-class cricket well before that. Retirement can often be a shock for people who have been used to fame and excitement, and has to be prepared for carefully.

Many retired cricketers go on to become **umpires**, to coach younger players, or to work for organizations such as their national cricket board or regional club. Some Test players have become commentators on matches on radio and television, or written about international cricket for newspapers. Others have tried much more unusual careers – Ian Botham once appeared in Christmas pantomime, while England spinner Phil Tufnell won a celebrity contest on television. On a more serious level, Imran Khan has become a leading politician in his native Pakistan.

After retiring from the game, cricket legend Imran Khan became the leader of a political party in his home country of Pakistan.

Sports psychology fact

All cricketers also have periods when runs or wickets are hard to come by. These dips in form can be made easier by coaching sessions which concentrate on ironing out minor faults in technique. Some players even consult sports psychologists to find ways of improving their motivation and focus.

Cricket records

Figures are a very important part of cricket. There are many different sets of figures involved in a game, from numbers of runs and wickets to numbers of overs bowled and batting averages. Most of the records here have been set since about 1980. This does not necessarily mean that modern cricketers are better than older ones. Cricketers (especially Test cricketers) now play many more matches than ever before – and a considerable number are against weaker opponents than in the past.

Men's First Class		
Record	Amount	Player/Match
Highest innings total	1107	Victoria v New South Wales, 1926
Lowest innings total	12	Northamptonshire v Gloucestershire, 1907
Highest individual innings	501*	Brian Lara, Warwickshire v Durham, 1994
Most successive hundreds	6	C.B. Fry, 1901; Donald Bradman, 1938/9; Mike Procter, 1970/1
Most runs in a career	61,237	Jack Hobbs, 1905–34
Most hundreds in a career	197	Jack Hobbs, 1905–34
Most wickets in a match	19	Jim Laker, England v Australia, 1956
Most hat-tricks	7	Doug Wright, 1932–57
Most wickets in a career	4187	Wilfred Rhodes, 1898–1930
Most keeping dismissals in a match	13	W.R. James, Matabeleland v Mashonaland CD, 1995
Most keeping dismissals in a career	1649	Bob Taylor, 1960–88
Most catches in a match (fielder)	10	Walter Hammond, Gloucestershire v Surrey, 1928
Most catches in a career (fielder)	1018	Frank Woolley, 1906–38

*not out

Men's Test Cricket		
Record	Amount	Player/Match
Highest innings total	952-6 **declared**	Sri Lanka v India, 1997
Lowest innings total	26	New Zealand v England, 1955
Highest individual innings	400*	Brian Lara, West Indies v England, 2004
Most runs in a series	974	Donald Bradman, Australia v England, 1930
Most runs in a career	11,174	Allan Border (Australia)
Most hundreds in a career	34	Sunil Gavaskar (India)
Highest Test average	99.94	Donald Bradman (Australia)
Most wickets in a match	19	Jim Laker, England v Australia, 1956
Most wickets in a series	49	Sydney Barnes, England v South Africa, 1913–14
Most wickets in a career	519	Courtney Walsh (West Indies)
Most keeping dismissals in a match	11	Jack Russell, England v South Africa, 1996
Most keeping dismissals in a career	395	Ian Healy (Australia)
Most catches in a career (fielder)	181	Mark Waugh (Australia)
Most Test appearances	168	Steve Waugh (Australia)

Women's Test Cricket

Record	Amount	Player/Match
Highest innings total	569-6 declared	Australia v England, 1998
Lowest innings total	35	England v Australia, 1957
Highest individual innings	214	Mithali Raj, India v England, 2002
Most runs in a career	1935	Jan Brittin (England)
Most hundreds in a career	5	Jan Brittin (England)
Most wickets in an innings	8	Neetu David, India v England, 1996
Most wickets in a career	77	M. Duggan (England)
Most keeping dismissals in a match	9	C. Matthews, Australia v India, 1990
Most keeping dismissals in a career	58	C. Matthews (Australia)
Most catches in a career (fielder)	25	Carole Hodges (England)
Most Test appearances	27	Jan Brittin (England)

World Cup Records

Record	Team/Score/Player/Match
Most victories	Australia (40)
Cup winners	Australia (3), West Indies (2), India, Pakistan, Sri Lanka (1)
Highest team total	398–5 Sri Lanka v Kenya 1995
Highest individual score	188* Gary Kirsten, South Africa v UAE 1995
Best bowling	7-15 Glenn McGrath, Australia v Namibia 2003

Women's World Cup

Winners/Record	Team/Score/Player/Match
1973	England
1978	Australia
1982	Australia
1988	Australia
1992	England
1998	Australia
2002	New Zealand
Most victories	Australia (39)
Highest team total	412–3 Australia v Denmark, 1998
Highest individual score	229* Belinda Clark, Australia v Denmark, 1998
Best bowling	6–10 Jackie Lord, New Zealand v India, 1982

*not out

Statistics in this book were correct at time of going to press.

Glossary

apartheid
policy that divided non-white people from white people in South Africa – officially abandoned in 1994

bouncer
fast delivery pitched half-way down the wicket which bounces shoulder height or above

crease
line marked outwards from the stumps

declare
close an innings before all ten wickets have been lost

drive
hit a ball near where it pitches with a vertical swing of the bat

edged ball
the ball can take an inside, outside, top or bottom edge off the bat. This can result in a catch to a fielder or the batsman playing the ball on to his stumps.

innings
passage of play in which all eleven of a team's players take turns to bat and score as many runs as possible. Each player's performance is also known as an innings.

leg side
the side of the field opposite to the side on which the batter holds his bat (i.e. to the left of a right-handed batter)

limited-overs
match in which each side has a set number of overs in which to score as many runs as possible

off side
the side of the cricket field that the batsman's or batswoman's body faces when they are receiving a ball

off stump
the stump on the off side of the wicket

over
succession of six legal deliveries by one bowler from one end of the wicket

pavilion
building which houses the changing rooms and in which the spectators sit

popping crease
line marking batter's safe ground in front of the stumps

run out
a batter is dismissed 'run out' if he fails to reach the popping crease when going for a run, and a fielder hits the stumps with the ball

stumps
upright wooden sticks which a batter guards during his innings. There are three stumps at each end of the wicket with two short sticks, called bails, sitting on and between them.

Test match
originally a contest or 'test' between two national sides

umpire
the referee in a game of cricket

wicket
1) the whole pitch on which a game is played; 2) the set of three stumps; 3) the dismissal of a batter

yorker
a delivery aimed to pass underneath the bat by pitching exactly where the batter's downswing will pass, but fractionally beforehand

Resources

Further reading

The Art of Captaincy, Mike Brearley
(Channel 4, 2001)
Secrets of leadership by one of the
best captains ever.

The Art of Cricket, Donald Bradman
(Robson, 1998)
The classic introduction to cricket
skills, by the master batter.

Coaching Youth Cricket,
Australian Cricket Board (Human
Kinetics, 2000)
A guide for adults and others who
want to run a youth team or just
coach youngsters.

Playfair Cricket Annual, Bill Frindall
(Headline, 2003)
A handy pocket book containing all
the previous season's first-class cricket
statistics plus records.

Wisden Cricketer's Almanac, edited
by Tim de Lisle (Wisden, 2003)
The cricketer's 'bible' – a round-up of
the past year's events.

Useful websites and addresses

These sites have a huge amount of
information inside:

www.cricinfo.com
www.cricket365.com
www.cricketarchive.co.uk
www.ecb.co.uk

England & Wales Cricket Board
Lord's Cricket Ground
London, NW8 8QZ, England

Scottish Cricket Union
Caledonia House, 1 Redheughs Rigg
Edinburgh, Midlothian, EH12 9DQ,
Scotland

Australian Cricket Board
90 Jolimont Street, Jolimont
Victoria 3002, Australia

Board of Control for Cricket in India
'Sanmitra', Anandpura
Baroda 390 001, India

New Zealand Cricket Inc.
PO Box 958, Christchurch, New Zealand

Pakistan Cricket Board
Gaddafi Stadium, Ferozepur Road
Lahore 54600, Pakistan

United Cricket Board of South Africa
Wanderers Club, North Street, Ilovo
PO Box 55009, Northlands 2116
Republic of South Africa

Board of Control for Cricket in Sri Lanka
35 Maitland Place,
Colombo 7, Sri Lanka

West Indies Cricket Board of Control
Factory Road, PO Box 616 W
Woods Centre, St John's, Antigua

Zimbabwe Cricket Union
PO Box 2739, Harare, Zimbabwe

Disclaimer

All the Internet addresses (URLs) given in this book
were valid at the time of going to press. However,
due to the dynamic nature of the Internet, some
addresses may have changed, or sites may have
changed or ceased to exist since publication. While
the author and Publishers regret any inconvenience
this may cause readers, no responsibility for any
such changes can be accepted by either the author
or the Publishers.

Index

Titles in the *Making of a Champion* series include:

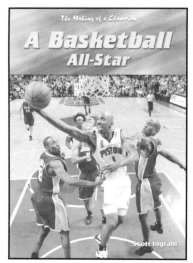

Hardback   0 431 18938 2

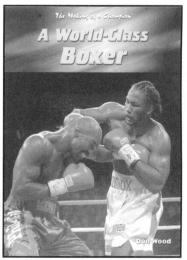

Hardback   0 431 18937 4

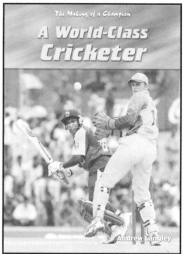

Hardback   0 431 18940 4

Hardback   0 431 18936 6

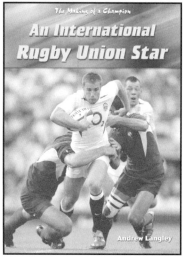

Hardback   0 431 18939 0

Hardback   0 431 18935 8

Find out about the other titles in this series on our website www.heinemann.co.uk/library